The world's largest golden teakwood mansion

P_{reface}

The book on **Vimanmek** is published to commemorate the Sixtieth Birthday Anniversary of Her Majesty Queen Sirikit of Thailand on August 12, 1992.

Vimanmek Mansion is believed to be the world's largest existing building made entirely of golden teakwood. It was built by King Rama V (King Chulalongkorn).

The following are quotations from the Bangkok Times Newspaper of Friday, February 23, 1900: *"Ceremonies were held in connection with the King taking up residence in the **Royal Pavilion** at Dusit Park..."*

The edition of Tuesday, March 25, 1902 said: "The religious ceremonies in connection with the King's taking up residence in the new palace at Dusit Park, commenced there yesterday. As is generally known, the new palace is the one which was formerly erected at Koh-Si-Chang and which has been removed to Bangkok and reerected..."

Her Majesty the Queen initiated the renovation of the long-deserted mansion in 1982 to coincide with Bangkok's Bicentennial Celebrations.

At present, Vimanmek Mansion, together with other buildings in its compound, is a museum of King Rama V's era containing many memorabillia and photographs of the period.

With Her Majesty the Queen's consent, the Subcommittee on Public Relations for Foreign Affairs for the National Celebrations of H.M. the Queen's Fifth Cycle Birthday Anniversary publishes this book in the hope of unveiling Vimanmek Mansion's unique beauty to the eyes of the world and enabling our foreign visitors to come to know Thailand's architectural style and cultural heritage.

The Subcommittee on Public Relations
for Foreign Affairs for the National Celebrations
in Honour of H.M. Queen Sirikit's
Sixtieth Birthday Anniversary.

Contents

Chudhadhuj Palace at Si Chang Island.

Vimanmek

Residence on the Clouds
The Genesis - Chudhadhuj Palace

H.M.King Mongkut (King Rama IV).

Chudhadhuj Palace.

The genesis of Vimanmek can be traced to a small island in the Gulf of Siam not far from where the Chao Phraya River meets the sea. The island is **Koh Si Chang,** and its potential as a royal holiday resort was first noted in the mid 19th Century by King Rama IV (King Mongkut) who attributed the remarkable health and long-life of its inhabitants to salubrious ocean air. On his private steamship, "Siam Orasumpol", he made periodic trips to this then sparsely populated island. For lack of suitable residence on the island, the King always slept in his cabin on the moored ship. On one of his visits, he bestowed the lofty title of **"Thao Kiriraksa"** ("Dame Guardian of the Mountains") on a senior and much respected female islander.

By the reign of his son and successor, King Rama V (King Chulalongkorn), Koh Si Chang's population had grown considerably; merchant sea-farers used its harbours as storm shelters as well as ports for exchanging and transfering their goods from ship to ship. It has also grown as a resort for royalty, and when the King sent his son, Prince Vajiravudh (the future King Rama VI), to convalesce after an illness, a precedence was set. It became the popular practice for convalescent members of the royalty to come to the island to recover their health in its pleasant surroundings.

In 1893 King Rama V and Queen Saowapha, who was advanced in pregnancy, took residence in one of the buildings erected for royal use on Koh Si Chang. Perceiving the rapid growth and potential importance of this island, the King decided that the Queen should remain for childbirth. On the 5th of July the Queen gave birth to a prince and on the 10th of August the King presided over three traditional ceremonies: the naming and blessing of the month-old prince, the naming of the

H.M.King Chulalongkorn (King Rama V).

H.M.Queen Somdej Prasripatcharindra.

H.R.H.Prince Chudhadhuj Dharadilok.

whole palace compound on the island and the laying of the foundation stone of what was intended to be the palace's main building, **the Mundhat Ratanaroj Mansion.** The baby prince was named Prince **Chudhadhuj Dharadilok,** and the palace was honoured with the name **Chudhadhuj Palace.**

The function of this island-resort palace was destined to an abrupt end in the following year when a political crisis in the Franco-Thai relations led to the blockade of Siam by means of the Gulf French gunships. Koh Si Chang was considered unsafe for royal sojourn, and Chudhadhuj Palace with all its buildings was never used again. The construction of **the Mundhat Ratanaroj Mansion** remained uncompleted. It was, however, not to be left to decay in disuse--as we shall see.

The Next Phrase - Suan Dusit Palace

Canals and islets in the compound of Suan Dusit Palace.

By the reign of King Rama V, the inner court which was the residential part of the Grand Palace had become extremely crowded with continual addition of buildings to accommodate its growing population. The Palace had become stiflingly hot during the summer, the passage of air being blocked by the closely clustered buildings, and epidemics—once started—were liable to spread easily within its crowded compound. The King, who enjoyed taking long country walks for exercise, often felt unwell after prolonged sojourns within the confines of the Grand Palace. He found relief in making frequent out-of-city trips (often incognito) to visit his subjects in various parts of the country.

During his European tour in 1897, the King saw the advantages of the European royal residences with spacious gardens on the outskirts of capital cities. On his return to Bangkok, he started the project of building a garden palace not too great a distance from the Grand Palace which constituted the nucleus of the city. Using his private

Southern gate. *"Tuaydhepsamosorn"* of Suan Dusit Palace.

funds from the Privy Purse, he bought several
connected pieces of farmland and orchards covering the area between Klong Padung Krung Kasem
and Klong Sam Sen, naming the area **'Suan Dusit'**
('Celestial Garden'). The first building in Suan
Dusit was a large single-storey wooden structure
used by the King, his consorts and his children for
occasional stay. It was inaugurated on 1st March,
1899, with traditional ceremonies and entertainments, and the King spent his first night within
the royal compound named **Suan Dusit Palace** --
later to be known as **Dusit Palace.**

The grounds of Suan Dusit Palace was divided by the King into individual gardens which
he allocated to his consorts and the royal children.
These gardens were irrigated and drained by canals, connected by paths and gates.

Surviving members of King Rama V's Court
still recall some of the whimsical names that the
King gave to these gardens, gates, paths and canals. The names were drawn from motifs on the
Chinese blue and white porcelain that was so much
in vogue with the collectors of that period. The
gardens were all named after well-known classical
blue and white designs, the gates were called after
those of the human figures and animals depicted
as parts of these porcelain designs, and the names
of the paths were taken from flowers found in
the classical motifs.

Beside opportunities for such pleasant inno-
vations. Suan Dusit had a more substantial fare for
the King's interest--an old monastery stood within
the new palace's boundaries, probably dating back

H.R.H.Prince Narisaranuwatiwong.

Happy lifestyle
in Suan Dusit
Palace.

Wat Benjamabopit

beyond the founding of Bangkok as capital. The monastery was originally called Wat Laem or Wat Sai Thong. It was renamed **Wat Benjabopit** (Monastery of the Five Royal Personages) after it was renovated by **Prince Pipitpokpubane** in the reign of King Rama III and later by four of the Prince's brothers and sisters. King Rama V decided to reconstruct the entire monastery, changing its name to **Wat Benjamabopit** (Monastery of the Fifth King). He enlarged the area and bordered it with canals. A religious ceremony was held to install boundary-markers marking the sanctified area, potential site of the new main assembly hall. The reconstruction of the monastery began in 1899 (it was not completed until after the death of the King in 1910). It is worth noting that the Main Assembly Hall of Wat Benjamabopit was designed by **Prince Narisaranuwatiwong,** the architect who created Vimanmek.

With its spacious compound, refreshing country air and moderate distance from the Grand Palace, Suan Dusit Palace was an undeniably ideal place for the King to relax after fulfilling strenuous demands of kingship during one of the most difficult periods of the Bangkok Era's diplomatic history. Beside taking his walks, the King also enjoyed a sport that came into fashion during those early days of Suan Dusit Palace--cycling. Having learnt to ride the bicycle in Sivalai Garden of the Grand Palace, the King often led his entourage on bicycle trips from the Grand Palace to Suan Dusit Palace, either spending the day and returning by nightfall, or remaining overnight at the garden palace.

View of Ruen Ton seen from Suan Bua.

The Rise of Vimanmek

$\mathcal{T}$he idea of building Vimanmek was conceived on the 19th of May, 1901 when King Rama V stopped at Koh Si Chang in the course of his visit to seaboard provinces on the eastern coasts and saw the uncompleted **Mundhat Ratanaroj Mansion** standing in the now deserted Chudhadhuj Palace. The King ordered the golden teakwood building to be dismantled and taken to Suan Dusit Palace where it was to be rebuilt as the main royal residence in the garden palace. The man who received the royal command to supervise this task was **Phra Rajayodhathep (Korn Hongsakul** -- later to become **Phraya Rajasongkram),** fourth generation member of the family that had served the Chakri Dynasty as master-constructors of royal temples and palaces. His great-grandfather, Hong, served under King Rama I since the founding of Bangkok as capital.

At thirty-five minutes past eight on the morning of Friday, 31st August, 1901, the King laid the ceremonial foundation for the building which

Ornamental plants at the royal greenhouse for Suan Dusit Palace.

Portico on the water's edge of the *"Jade Basin"*

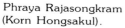

Phraya Rajasongkram
(Korn Hongsakul).

he named **'Vimanmek'**. The occasion was recorded in both the Royal Gazette and the Royal Command. A copy of the Royal Command for the Construction of Vimanmek was placed in the foundation along with traditional gold and silver bricks.

The architect of Vimanmek was the King's brother, Prince Narisaranuwatiwong. This beautiful structure was built in the shape of the Roman letter L with its two wings--one running westward, the other northward--joining at an angle of 90°. Each wing is 60 metres in length while the width in general is 15 metres, though certain parts are as wide as 35 metres. The height measured 20 metres from the ground to the fourth-floor ceiling or 25 metres to the top of the superstructure.

The building with its 31 apartments consists of three storeys with the exception of the octagonal end of the west wing whose additional fourth floor was used by the King as his private quarters. Though the lowest storey of the building is of stucco, the rest of the structure is made entirely of golden teakwood which is now extremely rare.

In the days of King Rama V, a large greenhouse complete with sprinklers stood just beyond the end of the west wing. It was said to be the nursery that supplied plants to all the gardens of Suan Dusit Palace.

Vimanmek is framed by four canals. **Klong Rong Mai Hom** (Groove of Fragrant Wood Canal) in the east, **Klong Karb Pan Krachok** (Sheet of Glass Canal) in the north -- now hidden by the wall that separates the grounds of Vimanmek from a compound belonging to Royal Thai Army -- **Klong Rang Ngern** (Silver Channel Canal) in the west, and best known of all is the large stretch of water on the south named **Ang Yok (Jade Basin)** because of the natural greenness of its water.

The construction of Vimanmek took only seven months to complete. Inauguration was held in combination with of top-knot cutting rites for five young members of royalty and the house-warming ceremony for Krom Khun Nakorn Rajasima who was moving into his new residence in Suan Dusit. Religious rites and entertainments lasted five consecutive days in celebration of the three combined events.

From this point, the King took up permanent residence at Vimanmek. The heyday of Vimanmek had just begun.

Vimanmek in Full Splendour

For six years, Vimanmek was the residence of King Rama V who found its clean air and beautiful surroundings a great deal more congenial than his former residence in the Grand Palace -- a fact evidenced by the following excerpt from a letter written of Vimanmek to his son, Prince Boripat Sukumbhandhu in the summer of 1901.

"I very much enjoy living here. If I were still at the Grand Palace. I would be finding the heat unbearable and would have to set out on another trip"

The king personally planted many of the trees to provide shades and greenness to create lush surroundings for his beautiful teakwood residence.

To the people, the King was no longer a remote monarch enstated within the all-enclosing walls of the Grand Palace, and the sight of the King travelling to and from Suan Dusit Palace grew to be a familiar sight to passers-by.

During the early part of his residence at Vimanmek, the King used the fourth floor of the domed octagonal part of the building as his private apartment. The floor directly beneath it was devided into two parts, the southern part was used by the king while the other was the apartment of **Queen Sukhumal Marasri** who acted as his private secretary. Below this was the octagonal hall serving as the King's living room. He often used it to receive private guests, and it is here that the royal barbers gave the King his regular hair-cut which was always ceremoniously performed in strict accordance with the ancient Brahmic belief that the monarch was a divine being whose hair must never be allowed to touch the floor. The rest of the building was occupied by the King's other consorts and his female children.

Beside this octagonal portion in the west wing, another notable part of the building was the loggia and its adjoining suite in the middle of the north wing. The loggia on the second floor was used by the King for his cabinet meetings. The adjoining suite west of the hall functioned as the apartment of **Queen Saowapha and Princess Valai Alongkorn** in the early days of Vimanmek. After Queen

Queen Sukhumal Marasri.

H.R.H. Prince Boripat Sukumbhandhu.

H.R.H. Princess Nipanoppadol arranging flowers at Vimanmek.

Vimanmek seen from the north-west direction.

Ngor Pa.

Saowapha and the Princess moved to another building in Suan Dusit, the King vacated the octagonal apartment on the fourth floor and came to reside in the loggia, using Queen Saowapha's former bedchamber as his dressing room. This was due to the loggia's convenient nearness to the Apisek Dusit Hall which was completed in 1902 and served the King as an audience hall as well as for his cabinet meetings.

The loggia became the birthplace of one of the gems of Bangkok Period literature, a drama in verse form entitled **"Ngor Pa"**. The work was written by the King during his eight-day recuperation from an attack of malarial fever. Unused to enforced idleness, the King passed his time by conversing with one of his page boys, **Kanung,** who was a Sakai Malay aborigine from the South. What the King learnt about the aboriginal way of life in the Malay jungles triggered his poetic imagination and **"Ngor Pa"** was the outcome of the King's convalescence.

It was said that during his illness the King would retire early while, a few rooms away, court singers and musicians would play and sing, allowing the music to float through to the King's bedchamber. The sound of the music would then be softened by the distance and the partitions between the musicians and the royal invalid.

The eastern wing of Vimanmek.

An interior view of Vimanmek.

H.M.King Chulalongkorn (seen in the centre) of the State Council in a room on the third floor loggia of Vimanmek.

The third floor loggia of Vimanmek was once used as throne room by King Rama V whose bronze sculpture is seen in the centre.

Satellites of Vimanmek

Apisek Dusit Hall

While the building of Vimanmek was still in progress, the King initiated the construction of a Throne Hall in Suan Dusit Palace for official use. Designed by **Phra Sathit Nimmankarn,** with **Phraya Rajasongkram (Korn Hongsakul)** as the master constructor, the long one-storeyed building is located east of Vimanmek on the opposite side of the 'Groove of Fragrant Wood' Canal.

Though small in size, Apisek Dusit Hall is an architectural gem. Exquisite details includes beautiful stucco motifs on the pediments, clerestory of multi-coloured glass and exquisite fretwork on wood that distinguished this architectural genre as belonging to the **'ginger-bread'** period.

Decades after the death of King Rama V, this Throne Hall was used as the Office of the Secretariat of National Assembly up to the time of the completion of the present Secretariat building to which the Office was moved.

Painted stucco Emblem of State in Apisek Dusit Hall dated Rattanakosin 122, the year of the construction of the building.

Intricate of fretwork at Apisek Dusit Hall.

Apisek Dusit Hall.

Ruen Ton

*D*uring the second year of his residence at Vimanmek, the King had a group of traditional Thai-style wooden houses built on the opposite side of the **'Jade Basin'** to the octagonal end of the west wing of Vimanmek.

It was his expressed wish to use this group of houses for the same non-royal style of living as that of a commoner. Here, he received the numerous acquaintances that he had made on his frequent incognito tours of the Kingdom. The guests, most of whom were commoners, dined on dishes prepared by the King himself and by the members of the Royal Family. The dishwashers were none other than the highest-ranking members of the nobility.

Ruen Ton

H.M. King Rama V with his working desk in Ruen Ton.

H.M. King Rama V's consorts and children at Ruen Ton.

The Twilight of Vimanmek--
The End of an Era

H.M. King Rama V in military uniform.

*A*fter six event-filled years, the vitality and bustle that enlivened Vimanmek came to an abrupt end with the departure of the King in February 1907. A dignified new European-style mansion is Suan Dusit Palace named **Ambharasathan,** had just been completed and inaugurated. It replaced Vimanmek as the King's permanent residence until his death three years later. Most high-ranking members of the royal family including **Queen Sukhumal Marasri** moved with him to live at **Ambharasathan** and **Udornpark** -- the latter being a much smaller building attached to Ambharasathan by a bridged walkway. Only some of the King's consorts and their children remained at Vimanmek where life continued in a subdued tone.

Towards the end of King Rama V's reign, Bangkok received two important state visitors in the persons of **the Duke Johannes of Brunswick and his Duchess.** Udornpark was vacated prior to the occasion so that the building could be prepared for accommodation of the European visitors. During this period, **Queen Sukhumal Marasri** and some of the royal princesses returned to Vimanmek to occupy the loggia on the third floor of the building. Their temporary presence breathed a short-lived glow of life into **Vimanmek's** now muted glory.

What had seemed like the final days of Vimanmek came with the deeply mourned death of the much loved monarch who had made this lovely 'residence on the clouds' a charming reality. **The King died on 23rd October, 1910 at Ambharasathan.** His remains contained in the traditional golden urn, were taken in a ceremonial procession from Suan Dusit Palace to the Grand Palace, the Official residence of the monarchs of the Chakri Dynasty. In keeping with palace traditions, the late King's consorts and the unmarried princesses returned to live in the Grand Palace, leaving the beautiful L-shape canal-bound building in desolate silence for no less than 15 years.

(From left) Queen Sukhumal Marasri, H.R.H. Princess Suddha Tipayaratana and H.H. Princess Napapornprapa.

H.M. King Chulalongkorn with his children.

Queen Indrasakdisajee.

Vimanmek's last royal inhabitant was **Queen Indrasakdisajee,** a consort of King Rama VI. Her stay lasted only a few months before she, too, had to depart -- as royal custom demanded--at the death of her royal husband in November 1925.

Since the close of King Rama VI's reign, Vimanmek served the function of a storehouse for the Bureau of the Royal Household. Its bygone days of music, laughter and courtly refinements survived only as nostalgic memories told and retold to the younger generations by those whose lives had been touched by the glory of its days of splendour.

During the Second World War, Vimanmek was hit by a fire bomb which fell through the roof onto the third-storey's floor in the north wing. Though its marks still remain to be seen, the damage to the building was very far from serious.

Like the fairy-tale princess, Vimanmek slept on through the inevitable passage of time that brought about so many amazing changes in the world outside its silent compound. Sometime during those forgotten years, the greenhouse that once stood beyond the end of the west-wing had fallen into decay; not a trace of it is left to be seen by the present generation.

The Present-Vimanmek Reawakening

*E*ighty-one years after its foundation was laid by King Rama V, the history of Vimanmek unexpectedly reached its full cycle. Touched once more by royal interest, it was to reawaken, pulsate with life and tell the story of its gracious past.

This turn of events came about in 1982, the year of Bangkok's bicentennary, when **Her Majesty Queen Sirikit** of the present Reign rediscovered the beauty and soundness of this forgotten building. Inside it, Her Majesty found a lavish store of historical and artistic treasures that were once the possessions of King Rama V and members of his family. With the permission of His Majesty the King, Her Majesty proceeded with the task of bringing the long-deserted royal residence out of the clouds of oblivion and unveiling its nostalgic beauty to the eyes of the world. The building was repaired, repainted and installed with new wiring system. By Her Majesty's command, the restoration was carried out with the greatest care to preserve it as it was during the period of King Rama V's residence.

On 5th October, 1982. Her Majesty the Queen presided over religious rites held at Vimanmek in dedication to its founder, King Rama V. It was, in effect, the beginning of Vimanmek's new cycle of life.

The present day Vimanmek is a museum of King Rama V's era. On the second floor are displayed the King's collections of porcelain and cloisonné, as well as tusks, horns, antlers and fascinating variety of beautiful walking sticks. On the third floor are exhibitions of crystal ware, pentachrome, and nielloware; the Throne Hall, the King's study, banquet room and the Thai suites are furnished to create the atmosphere of the era.

As for King Rama V's octagonal apartment on the top floor, memories of his presence are recalled by the use of the apartment's original furniture and the display of a selection of the King's personal belongings. It is composed of four rooms; his private study, bed chamber, dressing room and bathroom -- each furnished with great fidelity and devotion to historical authenticity.

Rows of ornamental plants stands on the site of the royal greenhouse of the bygone era.

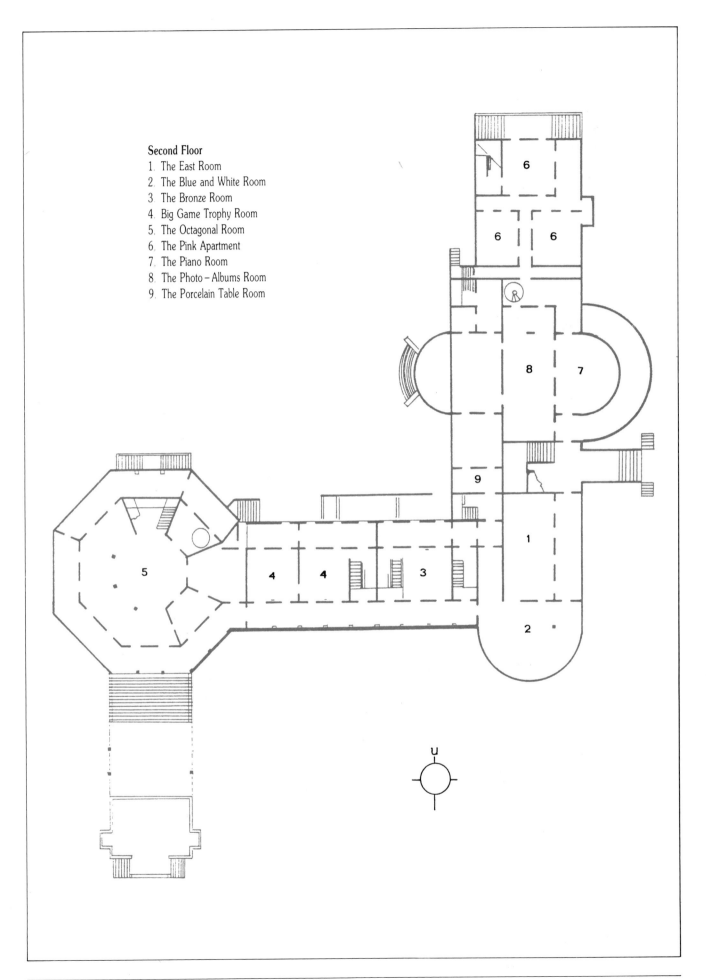

Second Floor
1. The East Room
2. The Blue and White Room
3. The Bronze Room
4. Big Game Trophy Room
5. The Octagonal Room
6. The Pink Apartment
7. The Piano Room
8. The Photo – Albums Room
9. The Porcelain Table Room

Third Floor

10. The Glass Room.
11. The Study-library
12. The Royal Banquet Room
13. The South Room
14. The Chinese Room
15. The South East Corner Room
16. The Neilloware Room
17. The Throne Hall
18. The Pentachrome Porcelain Room
19. The Miniature Room
20. King Rama VII Room
21. The Pink Apartment

Fourth Floor

22. The Study
23. The Bedchamber
24. The Dressing – Room
25. The Bathroom

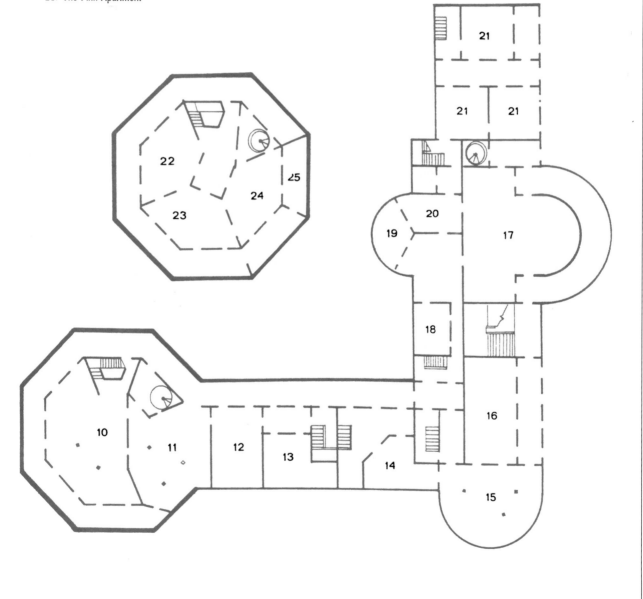

Show cases of silver utensils stand in an east room on the second floor. Photographs of H.M. Queen Saowapha and her sons hang on the right wall.

Blue and white Chinese porcelain custom made of H.M.Rama V with his initials as the motif are displayed in the south-west semi-circular room.

The doors opening out on this south gallery have a beautiful view of the stretch of green water known as Jade Basin and the group of wooden Thai houses named Ruen Ton.

This room on the second floor retains its old paint as it was not repainted during the recent renovation. Its exhibits are models of old ships and bronze statues.

Part of H.M. King Rama V's
collection of antlers.

กวางป่า(ผู้)
SAMBAR DEER

Bronze centre-piece in the octagonal
room on the second floor.

The octagonal hall on the second floor was originally used by H.M. King Rama V as his private living room. It is now used for displays of porcelain.

The exterior view of the Pink Apartment.

In the centre of the second floor loggia stands H.M. King Rama V's hand-carved grand piano. The Royal Seal of State is carved into its right side.

A full length portrait of H.M. King Rama VII presides over the spacious room west of the loggia. The glass cases in the centre contain albums of photographs taken in the reign of H.M. King Rama V while an assortment of silverware is displayed in the glass cabinets against the walls.

An altar in the tradition of Chinese ancestral worship with its blue and white porcelain set stands in front of the portrait of H.M. King Rama V. The Chinese Imperial Dragon is embroidered on the yellow silk alter cloth.

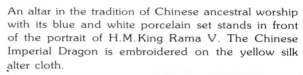

Portrait of H.M.King Rama V
in the East green room.

Thai classical music instrument displayed in the East
green room on the second floor.

Brass candelabrum with flower-shaped lamps decorates the ceiling of the second floor octagonal hall.

Fretted staircase spirals up from second to third floor in the north wing.

Southern views of Vimanmek seen from Ruen Ton.

Seen on the left of this picture is the loggia the third floor of which was once used by H.M.King Rama V as the Throne Hall. Next to it is the Pink Apartment, the residential quarters of H.H. Princess Consort Saisavali Pirom, the King's consort, and her daughters.

The octagonal room on the third floor now used for
display of glassware.

Portrait of King Humbert I of Italy painted by Rigoli hangs in the study-library.

This room on the third floor is furnished as a study-cum-library. H.M. King Rama V's writing desk dominates the room whose walls are lined with bookcases.

Carved dresser of Victorian craftsmanship in the royal
banquet room.

A chair in the Art Nouveau style that flourished at the turn of the century is flanked by photograph screens from the era of H.M. King Rama V in a room overlooking Jade Basin.

The *'Chinese Room'* on the third floor overlooking Jade Basin.

An assortment of Chinese blue and white porcelain displayed in and on top of mother-of-pearl inlaid cabinets.

Miniature blue and white porcelain collection in the 'Chinese Room'.

Another interesting corner of the 'Chinese Room'.

Signed photographs of Emperor Hirohito and Empress Nagako of Japan flank the southeastern room's doorway opening onto the east gallery. Below the portraits are rhinoceros horns.

The third floor room on the south east corner of Vimanmek contains H.M. King Rama V's fascinating collection of European and Thai objets d' art.

Carved cabinet containing neilloware.

Cabinet containing silver neilloware
in an east room on the third floor.

The third floor loggia was originally used in the early days of Vimanmek as throne room but later became the living quarters of H.M. King Rama V whose portrait is seen in the centre.

An elegant view of the spacious
Throne Hall.

The photograph of Their Majesties King Rama V and Queen Saowabha.

Ceremonial drum in the Throne Hall.

1

2

3

4

1. Chakri sets and other porcelain pieces are exhibited in the room behind the Throne Hall.
2. Carved Victorian cabinet.
3. Part of the royal pentachrome porcelain collection is shown in this octagonal cabinet with spiral decorations.
4. Ivory, silver and gilt miniature toys, much sought by collectors of that period, are displayed in the room behind the Throne Hall.

A room in the Pink Apartment which once belonged to H.H. Princess Consort Saisavali Pirom and her daughters is brought back to life with an emsemble of a beautiful Thai style four-poster bed, fabrics from H.M. King Rama V's period and a traditional Thai dining set.

Exquisite shrine enthroning Buddha image.

The Pink Apartment in the north side of Vimanmek is composed of four pink rooms used as the private quarters of H.H. Princess Consort Saisavali Pirom and her daughters. Thai-style four-poster bed, Thai fabrics of the period, and a traditional Thai dining set are displayed in this room.

Golden sunlight fills the anteroom in front of the King's bed chamber in his private apartment in the west wing. The apartment is composed of bed chamber, study, dressing-room and bathroom.

H.M. King Rama V's writing cabinet
in his private study on the fourth floor.

H.M. Rama V's dressing table with hand-cut crystal toilet set which belonged to H.R.H. Prince Maha Vajirunhish, the first Crown Prince in the history of Thailand.

Another set of H.R.H. Prince Maha Vajirunhish's hand-cut crystal set is seen on the King's dressing table in the bathroom.

Part of the building seen from the
gallery of King's apartment.

The southern part of the long gallery
that surrounds the King's octagonal
apartment on the fourth floor.

A tall tree dating back to the day of H.M. King Rama V stands in the centre of the picture. The stone path in the foreground leads from Apisek Dusit Hall to Vimanmek.

A marble statue, inscribed 'Al Lido' stands at the point where the west wing once joined the greenhouse which no longer exists.

The spacious portico that extends from the octagonal hall down to Jade Basin beyond whose smooth green surface Ruen Ton is visible.

A double vase of gilded red glass
Height 20.4 cm.

Toilet set of opaque glass decorated with the miniatures of His Majesty King Chulalongkorn, surrounded by floral design.

Jug	Length	30	cm.
Bowl	Diameter	39	cm.
Small bowl	Diameter	17.3	cm.
Covered dish	Length	21.5	cm.

Glass

*G*lass became very much in fashion in the reign of King Chulalongkorn. This was because at that time Europe was booming in its glass production: better quality glass was being produced, cut-glasses and crystals were of delicate beauty and apart from this, Bohemia of Germany had also developed and exported a large quantity of coloured crystals. The event stimulated much competition and expansion in the glass industries in various countries. In particular crystals: there was a development for faster production techniques, and there were also new glass decoration methods such as carving, colour-glazing, overlaying and cameo work.

Towards the end of the 19th Century, glass work in France entered the "Art Nouveau" era with the French Emile Gallé (1846-1904) as the founder. This particular class of glass work characterizes the deviation from the classical style to the unusual, colourful glazes.

Art Nouveau did not only favour glass work, it also gave new tastes to ceramics, jewellery, and furniture. The style became popular all over Europe, spread to the U.S.A., and commanded not a small share of popularity in Thailand.

The fine and brilliantly colourful glass from overseas seemed to meet with the Thai taste then. Glass wares were used widely, especially for floral arrangements for offerings during prayers, and there were imports of glass, made to order in the forms and shapes suitable for the Thai use. These included stemmed plates and joss stick urns.

Collection of glass became very popular during King Chulalongkorn's time, but for the unfortunate fragility of glass, there is not very much of any collection left nowadays. This booklet examplifies a part of the glass collection at the Vimanmek Pavillion, Dusit Palace.

Wine decanter, glasses and finger bowl, diamond cut with the initials of His Majesty King Chulalongkorn.

Wine decanter	Height	33.4 cm.
Water glass	Height	9.3 cm.
Champagne glass	Height	12.4 cm.
Red wine glass	Height	12.7 cm.
White wine glass	Height	12.1 cm.
Finger bowl	Diameter	12.6 cm.
Plate	Diameter	15.5 cm.

Red on white cane cut toilet set with the initials of Her Majesty Queen Sawang Waddhana in gilt on red panel.

Wash bowl	Diameter	34.8 cm.
Jug	Height	29.6 cm.
Perfume bottles	Height	20.1 cm.
		19.5 cm.
		17.5 cm.
		16 cm.
		14.3 cm.
		8.8 cm.
Covered jars	Height	13.3 cm.
		11.7 cm.
		6.8 cm.
Box	Diameter	6.5 cm.

Gilt and engraved plate and dishes
Plate Diameter 31.1 cm.
Dish Diameter 13.7 cm.

Green *Art Nouveau* vase
with silver design.
Height 20.3 cm.

Toilet set of finely cut bottles and boxes, the tops
are of enamelled silver with the initials of Her Royal
Highness Princess Valai Alongkorn, a daughter of
His Majesty King Chulalongkorn.

Large square bottles	Height	6.7	cm.
Small square bottles	Height	2.5	cm.
Round bottles	Height	6.7	cm.
Large box	Length	15.3	cm.
Medium box	Length	10	cm.
Small box	Length	9	cm.

Matching set of wine decanters and glasses plus finger bowl, diamond
cut, ending in v-shaped flutes at the top. All have the initials in gilt,
of Her Majesty Queen Saowapha.

Large decanter	Height 34 cm.	Red wine glass	Height 14 cm.
Small decanter	Height 24.7 cm.	Water glass	Height 10.6 cm.
Champagne glass	Height 13 cm.	Finger bowl	Diameter 11.1 cm.
White wine glass	Height 19.3 cm.	Plate	Diameter 15.3 cm.

Blue and white crystal bottle and glass
Bottle   Height   21.5 cm.
Glass   Height   9.4 cm.

Blue and white crystal toilet jars
Height   14.5 cm.
Height   10.7 cm.

Green perfume bottles with diagonal cut.
Large   Height   19   cm.
Medium   Height   15.3 cm.
Small   Height   11.4 cm.

Covered toilet jars in green with diagonal cut
Height 15 cm., 13.2 cm., 11 cm., 83. cm.

Blue and white crystal perfume bottles, the large one has a sprayer. Height 20.8 cm., 10.3 cm.

Art Nouveau vase with purple irises
Height 43.5 cm.

Unevenly tinted crystal bowl and jug
trimmed with silver, and silver serving
spoon and fork.

Jug	Height	20	cm.
Bowl	Height	18.3	cm.
Spoon and fork	Height	28	cm.

Bottle and glass of gilded red glass.

Bottle	Height	19.6	cm.
Glass	Height	9	cm.

Red vase with heavily gilded design.
Height 30.5 cm.

Tall vase with multi stems opening
into pink opaline flowers.
Height 50.8 cm.

A pair of *Art Nouveau* vases.
Height 25 cm.

Hand-painted Vienness decanter and dish with lid and tray, from *J and L lobmeyr Wien K.K. Hof Glaswaaren Niederlage.*

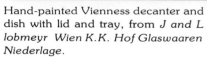

Decanter	Height 29.7 cm.
Dish	Height 13.3 cm.
Tray	Length 16.8 cm.

A large decorative plate with engraved signs of the zodiac around the rim and intaglio of nymphs and cupids in the centre.
Diameter 40 cm.

Jug engraved with floral design at the top and base and intaglio in the front.
Height 31.8 cm.

A royal presentation plate commemorating the visit of His Majesty King Chulalongkorn to the *Cantagalli* porcelain factory in Italy on June 11th R.E. 116 (A.D. 1898). Diameter 49 cm.

Porcelain

*K*ing Chulalongkorn's reign saw a significant diffusion of western civilization into Thailand. Reasons such as politics and economics have caused the welcome of these influences. The popularity of European porcelain during the period not only indicated the spread of western culture into our way of life but also expressed the shift of preference among the Thai people. The customarily popular use of the normally bought or specially ordered Chinese porcelain which has been in vogue since the time of Ayutthaya began to give way to European wares of different shapes and forms. This consequently somewhat modified the Thai eating practice from using the fingers to forks and spoons. Further, more European dishes were also served at various functions instead of Thai and Chinese food, which dictated the use of European wares and made European cuisine more known among the people.

Historically, the art of porcelain making began in China during the reign of the Han dynasty approximately 200 years before Christ and continued to be developed right through the T'ana (AD 618-906) and the Sung (AD 960-1279) dynasties reaching its successful peak during the Ming (AD 1365-1644) and the Ch'ing (AD 1644-1912) dynasties. It was during the time of the Ming dynasty that the method of producing the presently known "Blue and White" was discovered.

The process of Blue and White production involves painting the designs in blue on the porcelain then covering the painted surface with a transparent glaze and firing at a high temperature. The blue paint used at the time was made from cobalt oxide which when applied on to the porcelain, glazed and fired, gave the exotically beautiful blue pattern. This technique was developed right through the Ch'ing dynasty whose blue and white porcelain still remains to be seen in quite a quantity today.

This booklet shows parts of a large collection of porcelain at the Vimanmek Pavillion, Dusit Palace. Apart from porcelain ordered from China and Europe, the collection also includes porcelain from Japan which is another world renowned country for the art.

His Majesty King Chulalongkorn (King Rama V) had been an ardent collector of the Arts and had built up a large collection of porcelain which has been handed down as a priceless royal heritage.

Lattice work Royal Worcester porcelain tea pot, tea cup, and saucer with the portrait and initial of Her Majesty Queen Sawang Waddhana from F and C Osler, Oxford, London.

Tea Pot	Height	12	cm.
Cup	Diameter	7.3	cm.
Saucer	Diameter	12	cm.

Gilt patterned plate with the likeness of His Majesty King Chulalongkorn in the centre.
Width 21 cm.

Sévres tea cup with saucer, lattice work.

Cup	Width	8.5 cm.
Saucer	Width	14.5 cm.

Gilded porcelain coffee service with the likeness of His Majesty King Chulalongkorn.

Coffee pot	Height	25 cm.
Sugar bowl	Height	19 cm.
Milk jug	Height	12.7 cm.
Cup	Height	6.8 cm.
Saucer	Width	12.6 cm.

Egg Shell porcelain tea set, encased in silver, Staffordshire, England.

Tea pot	Height	13.5 cm.
Hot water pot	Height	18 cm.
Cup	Height	9 cm.
Saucer	Width	11.3 cm.
Sugar bowl	Height	7.6 cm.
Milk jug	Height	7 cm.
Oval tray	Length	59.5 cm.
Sugar tongs	Length	8 cm.

Lattice work *Royal Worcester porcelain by George Owen,* decorated with gilt pattern.

Tall jar	Height	15.5 cm.
Small Jar	Height	10.5 cm.
Square box	Height	9.5 cm.

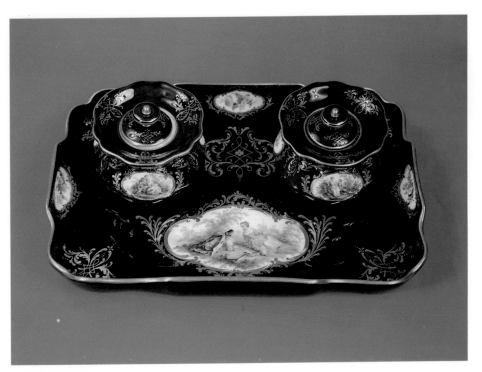

Dresden tray.
Length 28 cm.

Writing desk set from *Kaendler*. Dresden
Germany.

Round Box	Width	9	cm.
Bell	Height	9.8	cm.
Bowl	Width	6.8	cm.
Box-tray	Width	13.5	cm.
Oval tray	Length	23.4	cm.
Paper weight	Length	19.5	cm.

Coffee service by *Sèvres* or Vincenness
B^{lle} *Le Fonteroy* 1745 with the inscrip-
tion "Chateau de Tuilleries"

Coffee pot	Height	15.5 cm.
Milk jug	Height	9.5 cm.
Sugar bowl	Height	11 cm.
Cup	Diameter	6.8 cm.
Saucer	Diameter	12.8 cm.
Tray	Length	46 cm.

Wedgwood vase **glazed** and painted in
Art Nouveau style. Height 21.7 cm.

Sèvres blue glazed plate with raised gold
pattern on the border and the royal
initials of His Majesty King Chulalongkorn under the great crown of victory
in the centre.
Diameter 24.5 cm.

Gilded *Chinese style* tea cups with floral design made to order in Europe during the reign of His Majesty King Chulalongkorn.
Width 6 cm.   Height 5 cm.

Gold edged *Chinese style* tea set with silver gilt tray, imported from China, late Ch'ing Dynasty.

Covered Bowl	Diameter	7.5 cm.
Tray	Length	30 cm.

A tea set including teapot and tray. The cups are gilded both inside and outside and decorated with a floral pattern on the outside, late Ch'ing Dynasty.

Tray	Width	19	cm.
Cup	Width	6.5	cm.
Tea pot tray	Width	10	cm.
Tea pot	Height	7.3	cm.

Ornamental horse, Ch'ing Dynasty (A.D. 1644-1912).
Length 22 cm.
Height 20.2 cm.

Polychrome pottery with cabbage designs imported from China, late Ch'ing Dynasty
Plate   Diameter 53   cm.

"*Satsuma*" vase.
Height 40 cm.

Japanese "*Satsuma*" porcelain a craft which spread to Japan from Korea in the late 16 th Century. The cream porcelain is painted intricately in various colours and gold.
"*Satsuma*" drum shaped container.
Width 14.2 cm.

Blue and white porcelain container, Ch'ing Dynasty. *(Ch'ien Lung 1736-1795)* decorated in the early Ming style.
Width   16.2 cm.
Height   8.8 cm.

Blue and white vase, Ch'ing Dynasty *(Ch'ien Lung 1736-1795)* decorated in the early Ming style.
Height 24.8 cm.

Large blue and white plate patterned with various aquatic animals, Ch'ing Dynasty *(K'ang Hsi 1622-1722)*.
Diameter 50 cm.

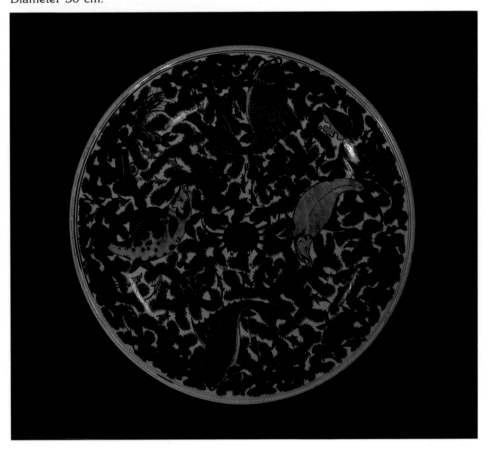

Blue and white vases with five clawed dragon design. Ch'ing Dynasty (A.D. 1644-1912)
Height 31.5 cm.

Polychrome pottery with "*khrut* seizing *naga*"
motif made in China in accordance with
designs and colours specified by Thai artists.

Covered bowl	Diameter 14.5 cm.
Plate	Diameter 11.5 cm.
Spoon	Diameter 14.5 cm.

Polychrome porcelain spittoons firstly made
in **Rattanakosin** period in A.D. 1880 depicting
scenes from Thai epics.
Diameter 13 cm., 11 cm., 10.5 cm.

Tiny ivory shelves.
Height 10.5 cm.
Width 5.5 cm.

$\mathscr{K}$ing Chulalongkorn's reign was a period in the Rattanakosin era when the country was in a comparatively peaceful and abundant state. The people had time to appreciate the arts and many luxuriate with the collection of Objets d'Art, such as blue and white porcelain, ivory boxes, glass works, and many other unusual artifacts. Once the collection of a certain art reaches the height of popularity, there would be exhibitions of the art where collectors would show off their pride pieces competing with each other, providing great entertainment in those days.

Towards the end of King Chulalongkorn's reign when His Majesty was staying at the Vimanmek Pavillion around B.E. 2445 (A.D. 1902), an Objet d'Art in vogue then was the ivory box.

His Majesty was taken by the tiny persimmon shaped ivory boxes used for keeping Her Royal Highness Princess Napabhornprapa's lip wax, and thought it was similar to men collecting pipes "Meerschaum". As men's pipes acquire the reddish glow after long use, so do the ivory boxes which shine with waxy translucent lustre after a time. What followed was a great fashion for new shapes and sizes of ivory boxes. The owner of a new design must have it registered, and there was high competition among keen collectors.

There was a magnificent exhibition of these ivory boxes at the celebration of the inauguration of His Majesty's daughter. Her Royal Highness Princess Srivilailak as Kromkhun Supannapakawadi at the Rajapridiwarothai Hall. It was an occasion still talked of with great joy and nostalgia by those who attended.

Ivory boxes and other small Art pieces collectively called here as "Collectibles" are those exhibited at the Vimanmek Pavillion. The delicate beauty of these Objet d'Art expresses the sophistication in the taste of the time together with the imagination and artistic flare of the makers and the royal collectors. The collection stands as a good witness to the feeling and attitude of the people in those days and should perhaps attract us of today to try to create that past, rich atmosphere.

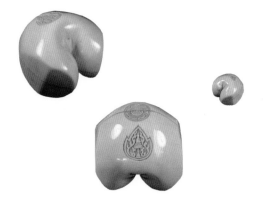

Ivory boxes shaped as antique
Thai *Coinage*.

Large	Width	7 cm.
	Height	6 cm.
Small	Width	2.5 cm.
	Height	2 cm.

Set of boxes on glass tray trimmed with ivory.

The pigs on the lid of ivory boxes symbolises the year of the pig in which Her Majesty Queen Saowapha and Her Highness Princess Consort Saisavali Pirom were born. The ownership of this set is still in doubt, for while the Queen was known to be a keen collector of ivory boxes, the pigs here are surrounded by a lotus motif that can be identified with Princess Saisavali Pirom whose residence was named Lotus garden.

Big box	Diameter	6 cm.
Medium box	Diameter	5.5 cm.
Small box	Diameter	5 cm.
Tray	Diameter	25 cm.

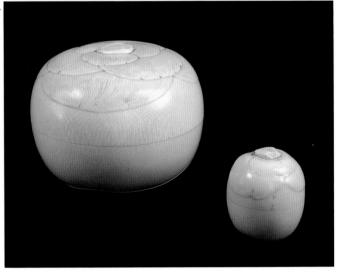

Drum shaped ivory box

Drum	Diameter	5.2 cm.
	Height	6 cm.
Base	Length	12.7 cm.

Ivory boxes shaped as *toddy* palm nut.

Large	Height	10.5 cm.
Small	Height	6 cm.

Thai *drum* and *tambourine* ivory boxes.

Drum	Diameter	3.3 cm.
Tambourine	Diameter	6.2 cm.

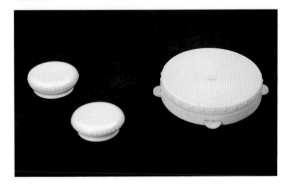

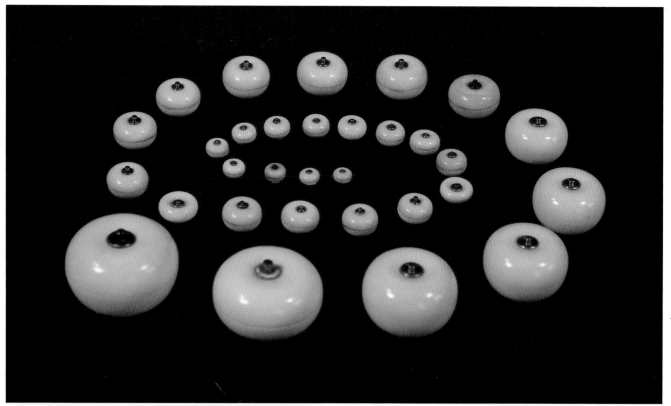

A set of ivory boxes in the shape of *persimmons*.
Diameter 8.5 cm. to 0.7 cm.

Set of betel leaf and areca nut boxes and a small mirror of ivory with the royal initials of Her Majesty Queen Saowapha on the lid.
Diameter 12.5 cm., 4.5 cm., 3.5 cm., 3 cm.
Mirror Length 5 cm.

Betel leaf and areca nut ivory box with the royal initials of Her Majesty Queen Sawang Waddhana.
Diameter 12.5 cm.

Ivory *Persimmon* boxes.
Diameter 4.7 cm. to 2.5 cm.

Meerschaum pipes :
Lengths No. 1   11.5 cm.
         No. 2   11   cm.
         No. 3   23.4 cm.
         No. 4   23   cm.
         No. 5   23.5 cm.

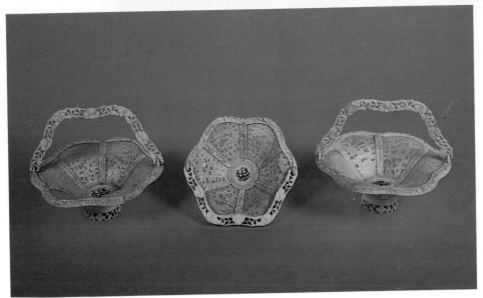

Ivory basket with open work carving,
Chinese craftsmanship.
Height 3.5 cm.

Carved ivory box with a mirror inside the lid
Height   7.2 cm.
Length 11   cm.

Ivory *Ball of thread box*
Height 4.5 cm.

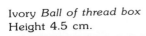

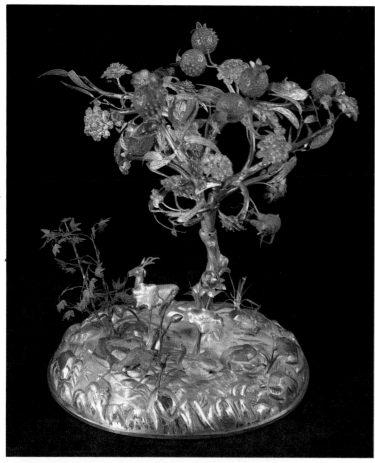

Miniature silver gilt dinner set and chinese hot pots.
Tray Diameter 9 cm. Height 3.8 cm.
Water bowl on stemmed tray with cup.
Height 4.5 cm. Spittoon Height 2 cm.

Miniature silver gilt dinner set,
water bowl on stemmed tray with cup.
Diameter 4 cm. Height 5.5 cm.
Pot Diameter 2.4 cm. Height 1.6 cm.
Spoon Length 3 cm.

Silver tree with woven gold fruits and an
inscribed plaque of presentation to His Majesty
King Chulalongkorn.

Agate baskets, with rim and handle of woven
gold and silver threads.
Diameter 11.8 cm., 5.3 cm.

French carriage clocks
Height 18.7 cm., 177.7 cm., 15.7 cm.

French carriage clock. Height 10 cm.

French carriage clocks
Height 19.5 cm., 7 cm.

Blue and white porcelain toy tea sets.
Tray. Length 15 cm.

Porcelain tea pot with water chestnut
handle, mushroom lid, standing on legs
of various nuts.
Height 11 cm.

Conch shaped tea pots.
Height 10 cm.

Paper-weight of diamond studded bird, sitting on an oak branch with pearl acorns. The gold base is decorated with diamonds and rubies. Length 9.5 cm.

Gold and Silver

The use of gold and silver for artifacts dates back to time ancient. In Egypt, royal household utensils were made of gold, and the popularity for the beauty and value of the metal has continued to be among the forefront both in occidental and oriental countries. For Thailand, gold has been used for royal household wares and for decorations for members of the royal family and high ranking officials. For lesser officials, the decorations are in gilded silver or silver, depending on the grades of officialdom. Even though Thailand was able to produce her own gold in earlier days at Bang Saphan in Prachuap Khiri Khan province, there was not much of it and it was very expensive, therefore gold has been used more in jewellery rather than for the making of sizable objects.

During the reign of King Chulalongkorn, Thailand developed an excellent relation with Europe through the two trips His Majesty made to Europe. From both trips His Majesty brought back handsome quantities of golden works of art of European skills, and in the time that followed His Majesty also ordered more of the European work especially those by the famous Russian jeweller, Peter Carl Fabergé. Today some of his precious works are in the royal collection of Thailand.

It is true that Thai gold and silver works possess long standing unique characteristics, but the Chinese skills for delicate metal work has also had much influence in Thailand, especially with silver. The popular Chinese silver works of the magnificently refined beauty was known as the "Shianghai Silver". Some of them had gold decorations and some were completely plated with gold for a more lustrous and valuable appearance.

Originally silver gilt was done by a method different from that of today in which an electrolytic process is used. The gold molecules are plated on to the object electrolytically for a comparatively shorter time than when the old method is used. This old method involves gold being powdered and amalgamated with mercury into a paste called "Piag Thong" (gold paste). The paste is then painted on to the object to be plated and a hot flame is applied to the painted surface to drive out the mercury leaving a plate of gold on the object. This method is also used in the beautifully combined gold and silver nielloware called "Ta Thong".

Gold and silver works presented in this book are a part of the collection at the Vimanmek Pavillion, Dusit Palace.

Water bowl on matching stemmed tray of engraved silver with enamel. Height 50 cm.

Snuff bottle and applicator of blue enamelled silver with the royal initials of Her Majesty Queen Saowapha with the commemorative wordings *"Presented to Her Majesty in the year of Rattanakosin Era 109 (A.D. 1891)"* Width 4.8 cm. Length 6.5 cm.

Gold cigarette box with a likeness of His Majesty King Chulalongkorn surrounded by diamonds on the front and a depiction of the royal yacht *"Maha Chakri"* on the back. It was made in imitation of silver cigarette boxes presented by His Majesty to members of his entourage in commemoration of the royal visit to Europe in RE 116 (A.D. 1899). Signatures of members of the royal entourage were engraved on each box. Length 12 cm.

A betel leaf and areca nut set made to order from J & W Benson, London, of pewter trimmed with gold, with the royal initials of His Majesty King Chulalongkorn in enamel.
Spittoon Height 13.5 cm.
Box Length 14.5 cm.
Betel leaf and areca nut tray Width 17.5 cm.

Gold cigarette box, the front embossed with elephant design decorated with diamonds. The back has the royal insignia of a crown set with diamonds. Width 7 cm. Length 14.3 cm.

Gold snuff bottle and applicator, decorated with the miniatures of Her Majesty Queen Saowapha and her children in the front. The back has Her Majesty's initials set with diamonds.
Height 6.5 cm.

Enamelled gold betel leaf and areca nut box with agate top decorated with multi-coloured stones and a set of small matching boxes. A gold and enamel spittoon.
Box   Diameter 12 cm. Length 6 cm.
Spittoon Diameter 9 cm. Height 6.5 cm.

Engraved gold box with blue enamel and diamonds.
Diameter 7.2 cm.

Engraved gold box of blue enamelling and diamonds with a clock set into the lid.
Length 9.4 cm.

Box of engraved gold with blue enamel decorated with diamonds.
Length 17 cm.

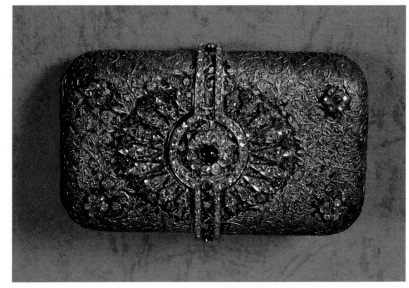

White gold cigarette box engraved into a design decorated with rubies, diamonds and amethyst.
Length 8 cm.

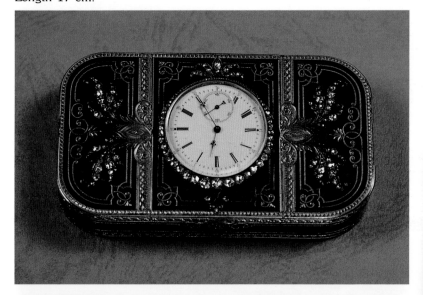

Cigarette box of engraved gold with pink enamel decorated with diamonds and a portrait of His Royal Highness Prince Bamrabborabak.
Length 11.8 cm.

Agate box with green enamelled lid decorated with flowers of diamonds and rubies.
Length 8 cm.

A box of *"narg"* (an alloy of approximately 7 k gold) with design of diamonds and gold.
Length 7 cm.

White gold cigarette box with pink enamel and diamonds.
Length 5 cm.

Gold engraved betel leaf and areca nut boxes with lids floral design of precious stones.
Length 6 cm., 5.4 cm. and 5 cm.

A set of four silver gilt betel leaf and areca nut boxes with agate tops and engraved design.
Large box Diameter 17 cm.

Silver gilt spittoon with embossed pattern of swans and blue enamel background.
Height 6 cm.

Silver filigree boxes decorated with gold and enamel, Chinese craftsmanship.
Diameter 13.8 cm., 5 cm., 4.5 cm., 4 cm.

Engraved silver gilt box in pumpkin shape, Chinese craftsmanship.
Length 17 cm.

Covered silver bowl decorated with the insignia of the first Crown Prince of Thailand, His Royal Highness Crown Prince Mahavajirunhish, son of His Majesty King Chulalongkorn.
Height 14 cm. Diameter 17.5 cm.

Silver filigree pumpkin with enamel.
Height 7.5 cm. Width 11.5 cm.

Engraved silver water container.
Height 44.5 cm.

Three layered food container of filigree silver. Chinese craftsmanship.
Height 27 cm.

Gold niello water container, King
Rama V craftsmanship.
Height 34 cm.

Gold niello covered bowl, King Rama V
craftsmanship
Width 10.7 cm.

Nielloware

"Niello" is an art of ornamenting metal objects much practised in the Middle ages. The lines of a design are cut in the metal, and filled up with a black lead alloy which gives effect to the intaglio picture.

The art is apparent both in Europe and Asia, particularly Portugal, England, Russia and Italy in Europe, and Iran, India and Thailand in Asia. It appears that the oldest evidence of the art is Roman, but the work is not exactly similar to that of the Thai niello, instead it is not unlike black enamel work and is called Tula silver. The Thai niello work resembles those from Persia and India and it can perhaps be concluded that the skills in these countries originated from the same source though have developed independently according to each country's culture and taste.

Originally the designs on silver niello were distinct with sufficient space for filling-in of the black lead mixture to give bold effect to the intaglio patterns. Later, however, people preferred a denser pattern, and there was also a development of a combined silver and gold nielloware. The totally gold niello came after that.

The silver and gold combination work is primarily silver niello with parts of the designs plated with gold. The plating is by the classical process of painting the patterns with a gold-mercury paste and subliming the mercury with a hot flame leaving only a plating of gold on the patterns.

For the totally gold niello, the material for the object can be either gold or silver. If it is silver, the designs can be completely gold plated instead of partially as in the gold-silver combination work. A nielloware is generally made of silver or gold since the lead alloy will not adhere to other metals such as copper or bronze.

Silver niello *mangosteen* style covered bowl, King Rama II craftsmanship. Diameter 6 cm., 5.5 cm., 3.5 cm. and 2 cm.

Boxes used as parts of betel leaf and areca nut set, King Rama II craftsmanship. Diameter 1.2 cm., 3.3 cm. and 3.7 cm.

Gold niello pill box with western style pattern, King Rama V craftsmanship. Width 8 cm.

Gold niello tray and covered bowl, King Rama V craftsmanship.

| Covered bowl | Height | 6 cm. |
| Tray | Width | 7 cm. |

Various gold niello wares, King Rama V craftsmanship.

1 Height	7.5	cm.
2 Height	7	cm.
3 Length	8	cm.
4 Width	15	cm.
5 Length	15	cm.
6 Length	14.5	cm.

Silver niello ladle of late Ayutthya craftsmanship and silver and gold niello ladle of early Rattanakosin craftsmanship.
Length 14.5 cm. and 14 cm.

Gold niello covered bowl, early Rattanakosin craftsmanship.
Height 7.5 cm.

Gold niello spittoons, late King Rama V period craftsmanship.
Height 9 cm. and 5.6 cm.

Silver niello covered bowls with gold tips, early Rattanakosin to King Rama V craftsmanship.
The largest   Height   6.5 cm.
The smallest   Height   3.2 cm.

Gold and silver niello bowl,
King Rama II to King Rama
III craftsmanship.
Diameter 20 cm.

Gold niello spittoon, King
Rama II craftsmanship.
Height 10 cm.

Gold niello aspergill and bowl on
stemmed tray, King Rama V crafts-
manship.
Bottle height   19   cm.
Bowl diameter   13.5 cm.
Stemmed tray diameter 12.5 cm.

Chinese style gold niello food container, King Rama III craftsmanship.
Height 34 cm.

Lotus style gold and silver niello
stemmed trays, King Rama II
Craftsmenship.
Diameter 20   cm.
Diameter 15.5 cm.

Gold niello covered bowl,
early Rattanakosin
craftsmanship.
Height 6 cm.

Gold niello spittoon, King Rama I
to King Rama II craftsmanship.
Width 33 cm.

Suan Puttan as seen from a distance.

The Museum Complex of Suan Dusit Palace

$\mathcal{D}$usit Palace, or Suan Dusit Celestial Garden was built like a garden palace for King Rama V, his consorts and royal children to use as a getaway place. The first building in the palace compound was a large single-storey wooden structure inaugurated on March 1, 1899.

The palace ground was divided into individual gardens, irrigated and drained by canals connected by paths and gates. While the King himself first resided at golden teakwood **Vimanmek** Mansion, and later moved to the European-style **Ambharasathan** Mansion, his consorts, royal children and members of the courtiers were allocated land to build residences within the palace compound.

On the north of the palace ground near today Rachavithi Road entrance, **Suan Puttan** is a section recently opened to the public. The section fell into the hands of the Army in 1932 when Thailand changed its government from absolute monarchy to a constitutional one. In 1990 Gen. Chavalit Yongchaiyudh, then the Army Chief, returned the Suan Puttan section to the Royal Household Bureau.

Buildings and structures in Suan Puttan were mostly in decaying condition then, due to long negligence. Major repairs and repaint were carried out to bring back the glory of the past. Seven mansions have now been completed and turned into a permanent museum displaying exhibition of photographs and items belonging to King Rama V's era.

Queen Indrasakdisajee

A land procession in which King Rama VII, robed in the full military uniform, is being carried on a Royal palanguin.

Suan Hong Mansion.

พระตำหนักสวนหงส์

1. Their Majesties the King and Queen preside over a traditional ceremony of blessing and naming their month-old son, H.R.H. Crown Prince Maha Vajiralongkorn.

2. A photograph of the Tonsure Ceremony.

The most magnificent structure of all in the newly-opened section is **Suan Hong Mansion.** The two-storey pastel green wooden house ornamented with exquisite openwork was the residence of the royal consort Queen Sawang Wadhana, who is the present King's grandmother.

The queen lived here after she returned from her convalescence in Si Racha in 1902. History has it that the queen was much interested in weaving that she set up looms and a weaving department in her palace and tried planting mulberry trees to cultivate silkworms. Due to the unsuitable weather in the city, the project was abandoned.

When King Rama V died in 1910, according to the palace law, all royal consorts and children had to move back to the Grand Palace. Mansions and buildings in Dusit Palace were shut down. Then Suan Hong was reopened to serve as a royal residence for **Queen Indrasakdisajee,** the royal consort of King Rama VI.

She moved from Vimanmek Mansion to stay here after King Rama VI died. After her occupancy, the mansion was completely neglected.

The recent renovation has brought back the grandeur of the past to this magnificent mansion. It now houses a display depicting old royal ceremonies and ceremonial processions for various occasions, plus an exhibition of old military uniforms.

Investiture Ceremony of H.R.H. Crown Prince Maha Vajiralongkorn, the son of the present king.

The Swinging Ceremony.

An oil painting of members of the Royal Family.

Suan Farang Kangsai Mansion.

A painting by an Italian artist, purchased by King Rama V when he visited Europe.

Suan Farang Kangsai Mansion stands on the very end of the palace wall. The pale pink two-storey building now houses royal accessories, portraits of the royal family in oil paintings and any items of historical value. Among them are a pair of coach lamps with elephant tops, unique pieces made to the order of Thailand when horse-drawn carriages were popular.

Other buildings further inside formerly belonged to members of the royal family including Princess Orathai Thepkanya, daughter of King Mongkut (Rama IV) and Chao Chom Manda Bua; Princess Bootri or Krom Luang Varasreshthasuda, daughter of King Rama III and Chao Chom Manda Eung; Princess Arunvadee; Princess Busabanbua-phan and others. These buildings are arranged into photograph museums.

Items used in royal ceremonies.

Museum I has no record of its original owner. Items on display in the three rooms downstairs are art objects from Thai and European craftsmen as well as photographs of King Rama V and the royal family. Upstairs rooms show exhibition on traditional Thai women costumes of the Bangkok Peroid.

A royal presentation plate commemorating the visit of His Majesty King Chulalongkorn to the Cantagalli Porcelain Factory in Italy on June 11th B.E. 116 (A.D. 1897-1898).

Museum I

King Rama V and Queen Sawang Wadhana, grand parents of the present king.

A gift presented to King Rama V by foreign dignitaries.

A photograph of 'Ngor Pa'

Museum II, H.R.H. Princess Orathai Thep-kanya Mansion, houses photographs of King Rama V in various occasions. Four rooms downstairs show personal photographs of the King himself, royal children and senior noble men. The first and second rooms upstairs are pictures of the King's visit, to Europe in 1897 and 1907. The third room shows pictures of his many foreign friends.

A picture taken by King Rama V

Museum II

King Rama V, members of the Royal Family and high-ranking officials pose for a photograph while visiting Europe.

King Rama V photographed with members of the Royal Family.

A photograph of Empress Mary of Russia

Pictures taken by King Rama V

A photograph of King Rama V
with one of royal princesses.

Museum III, Krom Luang Varasreshthasuda Mansion, houses a large collection of interesting old photographs. Downstairs rooms show picture of the first airplane from England to Thailand, the Regal Meeting in 1897, the Crown Princes of Thailand and King Rama V's sons among others. Pictures of special interest upstairs were those taken by the King as entries of Thailand's first photographic contest in 1905.

The King's keen interest in photography obviously boosted the popularity of the equipment and spelled out old beliefs that making any likeness of a person, be it in drawing, sculpture or photograph, would shorten the life of the person depicted. Many photographs taken in the old days have proved to be valuable historical evidences in the present days.

พระยารัษฎานุประดิษฐ์ ร ๕ นั่งเครื่องบินลำแรกที่มาเมืองไทย

1-2 King Rama V (standing on the platform) presides over the Tonsure Ceremony for one of the royal princes.

3 The elephant round-up.

4 A member of the Royal Family on a trial flight of Thailand's first aircraft during the Sixth Reign.

5 A royal prince leads a horse procession in the Fifth Reign.

The Royal Carriage Museum

part from old mansions in Suan Puttan section, a new addition to Dusit Palace is **the Royal Carriage Museum** where a total of 13 royal horsedrawn carriages used during the reign of King Rama V are on display. These carriages were refurbished to their original state and put on exhibition for the first time to mark the Sixtieth Birthday Anniversary of Her Majesty the Queen on August 12, 1992.

Horse-drawn carriages were said to be used in Thailand since early Rattanakosin Period. They were not very popular and available only for the Kings and among members of the Royal Family.

When King Rama V visited Europe in 1897, he ordered several carriages made in England to Thailand. **Chao Phraya Theves Vongvivat** and **Phra Nitespanich,** then Siam Consul in Singapore were assigned to find foreign-bred horses for carriage drawing royal procession.

The popularity of horse-drawn carriage continued in the reign of King Rama VI. The Royal Stable was set up to take care of both horses and the carriages. Horse-drawn carriages were in use until the reign of King Rama VIII. Automobile was introduced in Thailand and gradually gained more acceptance. The royal carriages were kept unused in the garage ever since.

The Royal Carriage Museum.

Glass State Coach Steuart Co. Culcutta.

Postilion Landau; Siam Import Co., Ltd. Bangkok.

1

The grandest of all carriages is the **Glass State Coach,** used by King Rama V to travel to the opening of the State Council session. Ornated with Thai designs, the coach was luxuriously upholstered in European fashion truely fitted for the royalty. The carriage is said to weigh about three tons, drawn by eight horses and manned by four postilions and two brakemen.

Next to it is the **Postilion Landau,** used in Royal Kathin ceremonies in the reign of King Rama VI and VII. While King Rama VIII and IX also rode in this royal carriage when they returned to Thailand.

There are also carriages of the court ladies to use in royal procession. These carriages were different from postilion landau for each is driven by a coachman from the box seat with four horses and two brakes. Another interesting carriage is the **Victoria Carriage** made to order from England. It was used by **King Rama VI** and **Phraya Ram Rakop** to present winner cup at the Royal Turf club.

2

1. English Landau; Siam Import Co., Ltd. Bangkok.

2. C Spring Phaeton; Alford Alder London.

3. 4 wheels Dog Cart; Lonesternon Holden London

Phaeton Buggy; England

3

SUPPORT Museum
Apisek Dusit Throne Hall

*A*nother building in the compound which was renovated is **Apisek Dusit Throne Hall.** Located on the east side of Vimanmek, it was built by the Royal Command of King Rama V as a Throne Hall for official use. An architectural masterpiece of the so-called "ginger bread" period, the long one-storey building possesses many exquisite details including beautiful stucco motifs on the pediments, clerestory of multi-coloured glass and charming openwork decorations.

When King Rama V moved permanently to Dusit Palace, Apisek Dusit Hall was the official Throne Hall where His Majesty granted audience and performed official functions. Decades after the death of King Rama V, it was used as the office of the Secretariat of National Assembly. When the present Secretariat building was complete and the office moved there, Apisek Dusit Hall was left into decay.

As part of the Queen's Sixtieth Birthday Anniversary Celebration, the government granted a budget to restore this throne hall to be used as a home of Thai art and crafts from the SUPPORT Foundation under the royal patronage of Her Majesty the Queen.

Apisek Dusit Throne Hall after renovation; now is a museum of Thai art and crafts from the SUPPORT Foundation

A bird's-eye view of Apisek Dusit Throne Hall

Crafts exhibited
at SUPPORT Museum.

Vimanmek
The world's largest golden teakwood mansion

Published (1992) by : The Subcommittee on Public Relations for Foreign Affairs for the National Celebrations in Honour of H.M. Queen Sirikit's Sixtieth Birthday Anniversary on August 12, 1992.

The subcommittee comprises the following members :

Mr. Chetana Sirisingh	chairman
Mr. Prathan Rangsimaporn	vice chairman
Mrs. Sundharee Srisomwong	vice chairman
Mr. Vijit Vuthi-Umpol	member
Khunying Dr. Pharani Mahananda	member
Mr. Rattanavudh Vajarodaya	member
Mr. Prasobchoke Onkor	member
Mrs. Sumontha Nakornthab	member
Mr. Chalermchat Tasukon	member
Miss. Sombat Bhuapirom	member
Mr. Nirun Ketkeo	member
Ms. Kawbua Chungsanga	member
Mrs. Pornsawan Utarnwuthipong	member and secretary
Mrs. Chintana Bhandhufalck	member and assistant secretary
M.L. Sidhichai Jayant	member and assistant secretary
Ms. Wanna Cholpraves	member and assistant secretary

Text : The third edition of "Vimanmek" of November, 1989, published by Public Relations Section, the Royal Household Bureau
 : Saowarop Panyacheewin

Designer	: Somsri Jamonman
Artwork	: Putiruk Sriouyporn
Photography	: Public Relations Section, the Royal Household Bureau
Colour-separated by	: Kanoksilp
Printed by	: Rung Silp Printing Co., Ltd.